Jess, Tom and Adam were friends.

Mrs Patel was their teacher.

One morning they all made robot masks.

They painted the masks in bright colours
and left them to dry.

In the afternoon Mrs Patel said,

'Now you can put on your masks
and be robots.'

'I am a robot,' said Jess.

'I am a robot,' said Tom.
'I am a robot,' said Adam.

'Can you eat like a robot?'
said Jess.

'Yes, I can,' said Tom.
'Yes, I can,' said Adam.

'Can you sleep like a robot?'
said Jess.

'Yes, I can,' said Tom.
'Yes, I can,' said Adam.

'I want the robots to stop now,'
said Mrs Patel.

'But I don't want to stop,'
said Jess.

'Stop!' said Tom.
'Stop!' said Adam.

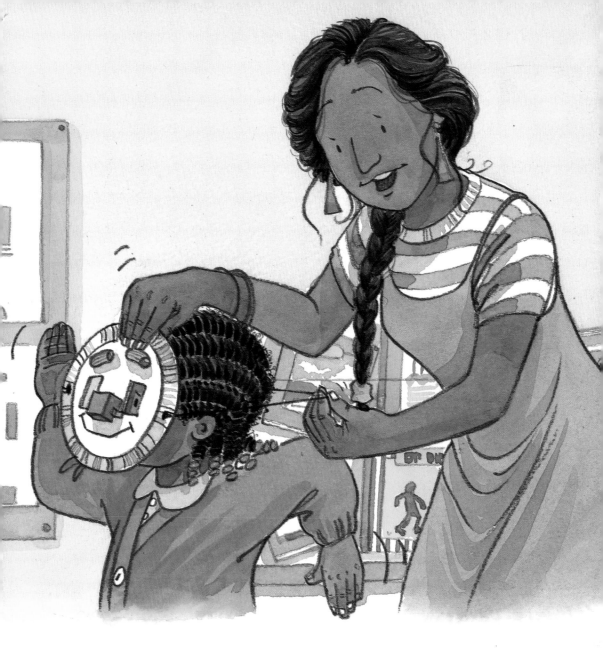

'I can stop a robot,'
said Mrs Patel.

'Now I am not a robot.
I am Jess,' said Jess.